DEFENDING OUR NATION

CUSTOMS AND BORDER PROTECTION

Series Titles

DEFENDING OUR NATION

CUSTOMS AND BORDER PROTECTION

FOREWORD BY
MANNY GOMEZ, ESQ., SECURITY AND TERRORISM EXPERT

BY
MICHAEL KERRIGAN

MASON CREST

Mason Crest
450 Parkway Drive, Suite D
Broomall, PA 19008
www.masoncrest.com

Printed in the United States of America
First printing
9 8 7 6 5 4 3 2 1

Series ISBN: 978-1-4222-3759-5
Hardcover ISBN: 978-1-4222-3761-8
ebook ISBN: 978-1-4222-8017-1

Library of Congress Cataloging-in-Publication Data

Names: Kerrigan, Michael, 1959- author.
Title: Customs and border protection / by Michael Kerrigan ; foreword by
  Manny Gomez, Esq., security and terrorism expert.
Description: Broomall, Pennsylvania : Mason Crest, 2017. | Includes index.
Identifiers: LCCN 2016053121| ISBN 9781422237618 (hardback) | ISBN
  9781422237595 (series) | ISBN 9781422280171 (ebook)
Subjects: LCSH: Border patrols--United States--Juvenile literature. | U.S.
  Customs and Border Protection--Juvenile literature.
Classification: LCC JV6483 .K473 2017 | DDC 363.28/50973--dc23

Developed and Produced by Print Matters Productions, Inc.
(www.printmattersinc.com)
Additional text by Kelly Kagamas Tomkies

CONTENTS

KEY ICONS TO LOOK FOR:

Words to understand: These words with their easy-to-understand definitions will increase the reader's understanding of the text while building vocabulary skills.

Sidebars: This boxed material within the main text allows readers to build knowledge, gain insights, explore possibilities, and broaden their perspectives by weaving together additional information to provide realistic and holistic perspectives.

Educational Videos: Readers can view videos by scanning our QR codes, providing them with additional educational content to supplement the text. Examples include news coverage, moments in history, speeches, iconic sports moments and much more!

Text-dependent questions: These questions send the reader back to the text for more careful attention to the evidence presented there.

Research projects: Readers are pointed toward areas of further inquiry connected to each chapter. Suggestions are provided for projects that encourage deeper research and analysis.

Series glossary of key terms: This back-of-the-book glossary contains terminology used throughout this series. Words found here increase the reader's ability to read and comprehend higher-level books and articles in this field.

VIGILANCE

We live in a world where we have to have a constant state of awareness—about our surroundings and who is around us. Law enforcement and the intelligence community cannot predict or stop the next terrorist attack alone. They need the citizenry of America, of the world, to act as a force multiplier in order to help deter, detect, and ultimately defeat a terrorist attack.

Technology is ever evolving and is a great weapon in the fight against terrorism. We have facial recognition, we have technology that is able to detect electronic communications through algorithms that may be related to terrorist activity—we also have drones that could spy on communities and bomb them without them ever knowing that a drone was there and with no cost of life to us.

But ultimately it's human intelligence and inside information that will help defeat a potential attack. It's people being aware of what's going on around them: if a family member, neighbor, coworker has suddenly changed in a manner where he or she is suddenly spouting violent anti-Western rhetoric or radical Islamic fundamentalism, those who notice it have a duty to report it to authorities so that they can do a proper investigation.

In turn, the trend since 9/11 has been for international communication as well as federal and local communication. Gone are the days when law enforcement or intelligence organizations kept information to themselves and didn't dare share it for fear that it might compromise the integrity of the information or for fear that the other organization would get equal credit. So the NYPD wouldn't tell anything to the FBI, the FBI wouldn't tell the CIA, and the CIA wouldn't tell the British counterintelligence agency, MI6, as an example. Improved as things are, we could do better.

We also have to improve global propaganda. Instead of dropping bombs, drop education on individuals who are even considering joining ISIS. Education is salvation. We have the greatest production means in the world through Hollywood and so on, so why don't we match ISIS materials? We tried it once but the government itself tried to produce it. This is something that should definitely be privatized. We also need to match the energy of cyber attackers—and we need savvy youth for that.

There are numerous ways that you could help in the fight against terror—joining law enforcement, the military, or not-for-profit organizations like the Peace Corps. If making the world a safer place appeals to you, draw on your particular strengths and put them to use where they are needed. But everybody should serve and be part of this global fight against terrorism in some small way. Certainly, everybody should be a part of the fight by simply being aware of their surroundings and knowing when something is not right and acting on that sense. In the investigation after most successful attacks, we know that somebody or some persons or people knew that there was something wrong with the person or persons who perpetrated the attack. Although it feels awkward to tell the authorities that you believe somebody is acting suspicious and may be a terrorist sympathizer or even a terrorist, we have a higher duty not only to society as a whole but to our family, friends, and ultimately ourselves to do something to ultimately stop the next attack.

It's not *if* there is going to be another attack, but where, when, and how. So being vigilant and being proactive are the orders of the day.

Manny Gomez, Esq.
President of MG Security Services,
Chairman of the National Law Enforcement Association,
former FBI Special Agent, U.S. Marine, and NYPD Sergeant

CHAPTER 1

INTO THE MELTING POT

From 1892 to 1954, millions of immigrants from nations such as England, Ireland, Germany, and Scandinavian countries entered the United States. During this time, over twelve million immigrants traveled through a small island in New York Harbor—Ellis Island, shown here in the early 1900s.

Across the world, the term *foreigner* often means someone to be feared and distrusted. In America, however, the notion of the "undesirable alien" is in a profound sense un-American; the United States has always been a nation of immigrants.

Often oppressed by poverty or political tyranny in their homelands across the oceans, our ancestors came here with the intention to build a democracy. Indeed, people are the richest resource of America, and diversity is a great source of its strength—as it says on the penny, E Pluribus Unum, "from many, one." In these dangerous times, however, such openness may also be a cause of vulnerability, an invitation to those who would exploit it for evil ends. Criminals, from small-time smugglers to large-scale narcotics traffickers and international terrorists, stand to gain the most through illegal entry to the United States.

Those who stand to lose the most are, ironically, the most recent immigrants, committed though they overwhelmingly are to their new homeland. Since September 11, 2001, and the attacks on New York and Washington, D.C., distrust of immigrants has—for the most part unfairly, yet inevitably—grown. The great challenge of our time is to hold the line against our enemies while welcoming our friends and fostering the international trade that is the economic lifeblood of our country. This most difficult of tasks falls on the men and women of the Immigration and Naturalization Service (INS) and the officers of the U.S. Border Patrol.

Words to Understand

Immigration: Moving into a country to live there.

Persecution: Harassment of people of a different origin or social situation.

Pilgrimage: Journey to a special or holy place.

A Home Away from Home

The Wall of Honor at Ellis Island is a place of **pilgrimage** for many thousands of Americans each year. For generations, this little offshore complex in New York Harbor was the gateway to America. Thousands passed through each day as ships disembarked their passengers from distant ports worldwide. Between 1892 and 1947, an estimated 20 million immigrants successfully passed through to a new life and new opportunities. Their descendants come to the wall today, to remember and give thanks.

Immigrants have made America what it is today. The immigrant heritage is shared, in some shape or form, by the vast majority of U.S. citizens, whatever their ethnic background. Even Native Americans originated elsewhere. In the course of the last Ice Age, they left Eurasia, crossing the "Beringia" land bridge (now the Bering Strait) to reach what is now Alaska. That was many millennia ago, of course; most of us can boast no such ancient roots in the land, being comparative newcomers, whatever our race or ethnicity.

The history of the United States is one of successive waves of **immigration**, as populations from different regions of the world flocked to these shores. Historians make a distinction between two different types of immigrants: those "pushed" by problems at home and those "pulled" by the attractions of the host country. The Pilgrims of the 17th century were classically "pushed"—religious **persecution** in their English homeland sent them in search of a sanctuary across the Atlantic Ocean.

Today, the Wall of Honor at Ellis Island in New York Harbor is a place where immigrants' names are inscribed at their families' request, for a small payment. The immigration station's main building can be seen in the background.

Other English colonists were "pulled," drawn by the prospect of rich and spacious lands for farming. African Americans do not fit into either of these categories, of course. They were effectively abducted from their homes and brought here unwillingly as slaves.

By the end of the 19th century, increasing numbers of immigrants were flooding in from eastern Europe, where Jews in particular were finding life

Ellis Island and the height of immigration (1890–1920)

Newly arrived immigrants pose for a photograph around 1910.

intolerable. The view that Jews were "Christ-killers" licensed their persecution throughout much of European history. They were herded into ghettoes and were then distrusted as a race apart. In reality, their only crime was to have fallen afoul of people's perennial fear and suspicion of what they do not understand—and this made Jews an easy scapegoat when things went wrong.

America may have offered a lifeline to all these immigrant groups, but the benefits have by no means been only on one side. The newcomers brought with them the skills (as craftspeople, farmers, artists, inventors, and so on) that they had acquired in their distant homelands. They also brought with them the immeasurable gift of energy. Their drive and enthusiasm gave enormous impetus to a fast-growing U.S. economy, an impetus that—thanks to successive waves of immigration—was ceaselessly renewed.

From Prejudice to Pogrom

In the empire of the Russian czars, anti-Semitism was a part of everyday life for centuries, and in times of economic difficulty, it flared up into full-blown pogroms. These were terrifying attacks against Jewish neighborhoods. Mobs vented their frustrations on what they saw as their ancestral enemy, burning homes and businesses and—all too often—killing people.

In the last decades of the 19th century, Russia's economic plight grew more strained by the year—and in the early 20th century, the country collapsed under the strain of famine, social upheaval, war, and revolution. This, combined with the continued violent persecution of the Jews, sent many thousands to seek refuge across the waves.

Jewish children in the streets of Warsaw, Poland.

A Worldwide Welcome

The Statue of Liberty in New York Harbor, a gift from the French Government, was an inspiring view for immigrants arriving by ship.

Generations of American schoolchildren learned by heart the lines by Emma Lazarus inscribed on the base of the Statue of Liberty— thankful for the spirit of welcome that first inspired them:

Give me your tired, your poor,
Your huddled masses yearning to breathe free,
The wretched refuse of your teeming shore,

Send these, the homeless, tempest-tossed to me,
I lift my lamp beside the golden door!

Text-Dependent Questions

1. How many people entered the United States through Ellis Island between 1892 and 1947?
2. What are the two types of immigrants according to historians?
3. Define a pogrom and explain why it led many Jewish people to move to the United States.

Research Projects

1. Research a famous immigrant to the United States. Write about what caused the person to move to the United States and how he or she became famous.
2. Research the top three countries from which people are immigrating to the United States. Select one of the countries and research to discover the leading reason people give for leaving that country and moving to the United States.

CHAPTER 2
NO ROOM!

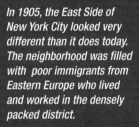

In 1905, the East Side of New York City looked very different than it does today. The neighborhood was filled with poor immigrants from Eastern Europe who lived and worked in the densely packed district.

A New World it may have been, but America was not necessarily immune to all the evils of the Old World. Even here, new immigrants encountered suspicion and prejudice. Like the countries of Europe, the United States had its economic cycles, its ups and downs—and immigrant workers welcomed in the good times might find themselves resented when recession came. Often, the worst offenders were those older immigrant groups that were yet to be finally established and whose own position seemed more precarious during economic downturns.

In the 19th century, a new understanding emerged. Although a country as vast as the United States might, in theory, have room for all, a modern, democratic society can develop only if all citizens are documented and all new arrivals registered in an orderly fashion. The American welcome could hardly be expected to extend to hardened criminals or those suspected of being agents of hostile foreign governments, while dangerous diseases had to be excluded for the good of all. The floodgates, if not closed, were clearly going to have to be more carefully supervised. Serious immigration control was accordingly undertaken from the last decade of the 19th century.

Breathing Free?

Life was not necessarily comfortable for the country's immigrants. The possibilities of American life may have been limitless in the longer term, but most new immigrants found their immediate prospects severely restricted as they struggled to survive in the poorest quarters of a few

Words to Understand

Internment: Confinement of a person or group of people during war.

Racism: The belief that one race is superior to another.

Scapegoat: Person blamed for a problem or situation caused by someone else.

big cities. Even in boom-times when jobs were available, there was always an abundance of U.S.-born labor competing to claim them, and when the crash came, there were always Americans on the lookout for an alien **scapegoat** to blame for their troubles. It was becoming clear that immigration required some measures of control to protect not only Americans but also the immigrants themselves.

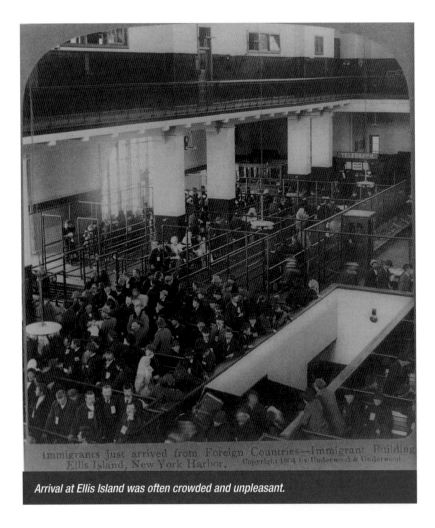

Immigrants just arrived from Foreign Countries—Immigrant Building
Ellis Island, New York Harbor.   Copyright 1904 by Underwood & Underwood

Arrival at Ellis Island was often crowded and unpleasant.

The first serious acknowledgment at an official level that the flow of incomers to the United States would have to be policed and carefully controlled came in the 1880s. Despite the best of intentions, the new bureaucracy became an object of fear for incoming immigrants; its methods were not always either sensitive or compassionate by modern standards. However fondly it is visited now by their descendants, the "clearing station" on Ellis Island was regarded with considerable dread by the immigrants themselves, for entrance to America was by no means assured. After an intrusively thorough interrogation and an often humiliating physical examination, many were turned back from the country's doorstep on account of officials' (sometimes groundless) suspicions that they were bearing infectious disease or had irregularities in their papers.

For those excluded—at times as many as 20 percent of all applicants—there remained only the heartbreaking prospect of a return to what might now be a hostile "home." The prevailing atmosphere in a center where as many as 8,500 might be processed in a single day was, accordingly, one of bewildering confusion mingled with hope and—above all—profound anxiety. "To me it was like the House of Babel," Russian-born Barbara Barondess would recall a lifetime later. "There were so many languages and so many people. And everybody huddled together. And it was so full of fear, it was pathetic."

A West Coast Welcome

Angel Island, in San Francisco Bay, served a comparable purpose for immigrants on America's West Coast. Many thousands of Chinese and other Asian immigrants passed through the center here. "I was really scared," admitted Jin Hua in a letter to her school friend at home, Xiao Hong, in 1881. "Until this point, I had never seen such a variety of faces and skin colors. What if I get lost? What if something is wrong with me? What if I do not pass their tests? What if I am sent back? The what-ifs kept going through my head. Finally, after six hours, it was my turn to be checked. The inspector looked at me like some sort of strange bug. He checked my luggage (I had only one small trunk) as if he expected to find weapons in it. The man looked almost angry when the only things that he could find were my clothes—he checked those too—some books, and a photograph of my family. He took all the books even though I tried to explain that they were required for college."

What Are Americans?

Though in most respects an enthusiast for all things American, college student Jin Hua could still write sadly to a friend back in China, "Sometimes I feel that I do not belong here." She could hardly be blamed for having mixed feelings, given U.S. officialdom's apparent ambivalence toward her fellow Chinese. "A law was passed recently,"

The Angel Island Immigration Station— gateway to America for immigrants from the Pacific from 1910 to 1940.

she notes in a letter sent to her friend Xiao Hong in 1882, "that no Chinese can enter or exit the United States for the next 10 years." These were indeed the terms of that year's Chinese Exclusion Act; legislation in this period seldom bothered to conceal racist assumptions that did not shame white America at this time. The passing of the Immigration Act of 1891 put the rules on a more formal footing, but did nothing to change their discriminatory character. The Immigration Act of 1917, the Quota Act of 1921, and the Johnson-Reed Act of 1924 were unabashedly aimed at the exclusion of any but white northern and western European immigrants.

Racism is still very much a problem in America, as it is in other modern societies— although now, at least, it is generally regarded as a social evil. In the late 19th and early 20th centuries, however, racism was considered to be a thoroughgoing, scientific theory. If immigration control now has a bad name among some sections of the population, this is in large part due to the earlier prejudices and abuses of that time. Supposedly rigorous IQ (intelligence quotient) testing branded some races "less intelligent" than others. No allowance was made for the effect of cultural and linguistic factors on the findings of ineptly constructed tests. Put simply, white Anglo-Saxon immigrants passed these tests more easily than did other groups— especially non-Europeans. Immigrants from northern Europe found it easy to answer questions "correctly" when that "correctness" was very much dependent on a white Anglo-Saxon way of thinking. Other "researchers" ingeniously "proved" the superiority of the European to the

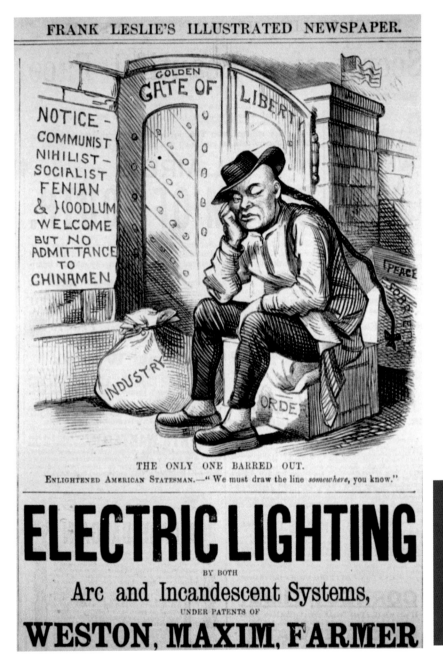

Asiatic and African brain, arguing that white people were further evolved from their primeval "apehood." Such pseudoscience now stands completely discredited, of course; modern geneticists have left its findings in tatters. But the damage it did in its day was profound, and its consequences endure.

Where Two Worlds Meet

Once, they came "tempest-tossed" from the "teeming shores" of Europe; now they trek north from the villages of Chiapas and beyond. But the same age-old economic forces are still "pushing" immigrants in the direction of America, a constant headache for those entrusted with the task of keeping order along the borders. Victor Manjarrez of the Naco, AZ, Border Patrol is himself a Mexican American, and he is realistic about the endless streams of would-be immigrants attempting to cross our southern frontier illegally. "I think," he told *Time*'s Terry McCarthy, "we in the Border Patrol are getting better at what we are doing. But with a Third World economy to the south and a First World economic power to the north, we will always have this problem."

Racism has also led to other misjudgments—the **internment** of Japanese Americans at the time of the Second World War, for instance—not to mention the long and bloody struggle endured by African Americans to claim their civil rights in U.S. society. Yet, although America was initially slow to recognize its racism, it has striven in recent decades to make amends. The majority of Americans today are tolerant, as befits a nation of immigrants. Even now there may be tensions, however. Indeed, we see the old cycles still at work, with immigrants welcomed as cheap labor for farmers or affluent urban householders in the good times and resented as a drain on the resources of the nation when times are hard.

Despite these undoubted difficulties, all the indications are that immigrants will continue to settle in America—even if it may be a struggle to become established—while America will continue to thrive, thanks to their contributions. If any refutation were needed of the grotesque absurdity of racist thinking, it is to be found in the extraordinary achievements of that unrivaled world superpower, which might just as accurately be called the United Races of America.

A mother stands with her two children outside their home at the Manzanar Relocation Center.

Text-Dependent Questions

1. When did the government first begin to police and control immigration to the United States?
2. What was the Chinese Exclusion Act?
3. Name one effect of racism against immigrants to the United States.

Research Projects

1. Research the Chinese Exclusion Act. What prompted its enactment? How did the U.S. population react? Does the U.S. Constitution support it?
2. Research the internment of Japanese people in the United States during World War II.
3. When did it begin? What prompted it? How many Japanese Americans were interned? How were these people treated during their internment?

CHAPTER 3
THE MODERN MIGRANTS

Chinatown in New York City is one of the oldest Chinese ethnic enclaves, containing the largest ethnic Chinese population outside of Asia.

A merica remains very much a nation of immigrants, with many thousands arriving every year, following in the footsteps of those who made their way during the 19th and 20th centuries.

Stragglers from Britain and Ireland, Italy, the Scandinavian countries, and eastern Europe still come to join well-established immigrant communities, and new waves of immigrants are flooding in from the Caribbean and Latin America. Many more have come across the Pacific from countries such as China, Vietnam, the Philippines, and India. As before, some are "pulled" by the

---

Safe at Last: Zo T. Hmung

The brutal coup of 1962 put an end to democracy in the Asian state of Burma—for the Chin people it also brought religious persecution. A Christian minority in a predominantly Buddhist state, they were regarded with especial suspicion by a military government that was ruthless toward those it saw as troublemakers. When the Burmese pro-democracy movement took off from 1988 onward, many Chin played an enthusiastic part. One such, Zo T. Hmung, campaigned underground in Burma for several years, but was eventually forced to flee across the border into India, where thousands of exiled Burmese were already living.

In 1994, however, the Burmese and Indian governments signed a cross-border cooperation agreement, under the terms of which many hundreds of Burmese refugees were to be rounded up and summarily returned to their homeland—and to the none-too-tender mercies of an angry government. Facing the prospect of returning home to a certain death, Zo T. Hmung fled again, this time to the United States, where he was granted political asylum.

Continuing his campaign for democracy in Burma, he was shocked to learn that, back in India, his wife and children were on the brink of being returned home—where they would effectively be hostages of the Burmese government. Thanks to the intervention of a number of agencies, they were released by the Indian authorities. The family was joyfully reunited at New York's John F. Kennedy Airport, to begin a new life in the United States.

Words to Understand

Congregate: Assemble as a crowd or mass.

Emigration: Leaving a country to live in another one.

Segregationist: Person who supports separation according to race.

A U.S. Border Patrol agent inspects vehicles at a border checkpoint in California.

prospect of a better life; others are "pushed" by political upheaval or war in their home country. America continues to offer sanctuary to many who might otherwise be in danger from dictators and their agents of torture elsewhere in the world. Today, although there may be tensions, Americans have a far better understanding of immigrants' contribution to the national life—their ability to make our nation more culturally colorful and also more prosperous. Immigrants are,

by definition, individuals of energy and enterprise: the whole nation gains from their hard work and creativity.

Facts and Figures

Each year, enough immigrants to populate a city settle legally in the United States. The figure for 2014 was 1,016,518. The number of illegal entrants can only be estimated. According to a 2014 Pew Research Study, there are approximately 11 million undocumented immigrants. Five countries accounted for approximately 39 percent of America's legal immigrants in 2014: Mexico (133,107), the People's Republic of China (72,492), the Philippines (48,663), India (74,451), and Vietnam (29,825). Between 2000 and 2014 the numbers of people arriving from China and India almost doubled. Mexico is believed to be the largest single source of illegal immigrants. An estimated 6.4 million undocumented Mexicans live here. A long way after this come El Salvador with 335,000, Guatemala with 165,000, and Canada with 120,000, by best current estimates. Haiti follows with 105,000 and the Philippines with 95,000. Other countries are represented too, from Ireland to India, and from Peru to Poland.

Making Good

Koreatown in Los Angeles.

A Korean immigrant in New Jersey, Haesu Choi spends two to three hours each evening giving her two sons, ages 10 and 8, extra coaching with their schoolwork. "They complain that their friends get to watch TV," she told Heather MacDonald of the New York *City Journal*. "But I tell them, because we're Asian, they have to do better." To the great benefit of America throughout its history, successive immigrant groups have all been driven by a desire to succeed—but even by these standards the Koreans are special.

Though many have come to America with university educations, they have been prepared to work long hours for low wages in menial trades. Slowly, they have come to thrive. No fewer than 20 percent of America's dry-cleaning businesses are now Korean-owned. In southern California, 45 percent of the liquor stores and 46 percent of small supermarkets belong to Koreans, while in parts of Manhattan, they own 75 percent of the grocery stores. Koreans have been a presence in America for over a century, but in the past few decades their numbers have grown, with substantial Koreatowns springing up in several cities—most notably Los Angeles.

All these figures should be set against those for **emigration**. Thousands of legal immigrants change their minds and decide to return to their home countries every year, while U.S.-born citizens leave to pursue lives and careers elsewhere. Despite this, however, the net trend is clearly upward. Large as these numbers are, they would have little impact if evenly dispersed throughout the United States. Immigration, however, tends to be concentrated around several major centers. Of legal immigrants into America in 2000, for instance, some 68 percent settled in six key states: California, Texas, Florida, New York, New Jersey, and Illinois.

The New Americans

Today's immigrants may come from very different parts of the world than their predecessors and from very different cultural backgrounds, but their response to the immigrant experience has been strikingly similar. They have tended to **congregate** in particular quarters to keep one another company in a strange society. For instance, New York's Chinatown and Little Italy have been joined by a distinctly Korean K-Town; while Miami's Little Havana is famous the world over.

These new Americans also share with their immigrant predecessors an indomitable work ethic and the will to succeed in the face of challenges that would discourage more established, more comfortable communities. Immigrants have historically been willing to work long hours, forgoing luxuries and leisure time, to give their children the benefits of a better life. The spirit of self-help runs deep in immigrant communities. Far from "milking" welfare or health care services, the opposite appears to be the case. Work by the National Academy of Sciences clearly showed that the average immigrant pays $1,800 more in taxes than he or she receives in benefits each year. A study published by the Institute on Taxation and Economic Policy estimated in 2016 that illegal immigrants contribute as much as $12 billion each year in state and local taxes in the form of income, property, or sales taxes.

A Long Journey

Isaac Borenstein's life story provides a short course in 20th-century history. His family lived in Poland before World War II. Most of his relations were destined to be murdered in the Nazi Holocaust, but Borenstein's branch of the family fled to Havana, Cuba, where Isaac was born in 1950. When Fidel Castro's Communists took power, they were forced to flee again—this time to the United States, to Nashville, TN.

What he found in the segregationist South both confused and shocked the young immigrant. As both a Jew and a Spanish-speaker, he felt rejected; and the "whites only" water fountains were, he felt, an ugly stain on a "wonderful country." Determined to serve both his adoptive country and the cause of justice, he studied law, and, beginning in 1986, served as a judge in Boston. He retired in September 2008 but continues to work as an attorney and is an adjunct professor of law at Suffolk Law School.

Borenstein sees America's imperfections clearly, but in the end there is nowhere else he would want to be. "I'm very corny about democracy," he admitted to Stan Grossfeld of *The Boston Globe Magazine*. This is his homeland, he says: "I'm incredibly proud and grateful."

However much the immigrants may gain from America, then, America gets more in return—even in the most down-to-earth economic terms. Once the calculation is extended to include such intangibles as the energy and ingenuity of the immigrants, the balance of benefits shifts overwhelmingly in America's favor.

Ingenious Immigrants

The economic contribution made by immigrants is clear, but what about the claim that they contribute creativity and enterprise to their adoptive country? Some years ago, to test the

New American citizens take the citizenship oath in St. Petersburg, FL.

Mexican American farmworkers tend rows of potatoes on this large Central California farm.

truth of this theory, the Alexis de Tocqueville Institution (AdTI) conducted a novel study that worked out the proportion of U.S. patents taken out by immigrants to the country. Analysis of the patents registered gives researchers a snapshot of cutting-edge technology at any given time. Taking 250 randomly selected recent patents, the AdTI went on to trace the background of the inventors, discovering that 48 out of 250—or 19 percent—were immigrants. As a proportion of the U.S. population, recent immigrants represent only 8.7 percent, so the implication is that they are contributing over twice their share.

New immigrants to America and what drove them to leave behind the lives they knew.

A Place of Safety

Of those granted U.S. citizenship in 2014, 134,242 were classed as either refugees or asylum seekers—people forced to flee their homelands by political developments there. With so many wars in the world and with so many tyrannical regimes, there are many men and women with what the Statute of the United Nations High Commissioner for Refugees (UNHCR) calls "a well-founded fear of persecution." Governments have, by international agreement, a legal duty to provide political asylum for those in this position—although asylum seekers must first satisfy their prospective host that their "fear of persecution" is indeed "well-founded."

In the United States prior to 2003, the Immigration and Naturalization Service (INS) was responsible for ruling on applications in what had become an increasingly controversial area. Across the developed world, asylum applicants have been regarded with increasing suspicion by those who believe they may be motivated more by a desire for economic betterment than by genuine persecution. The fear that public goodwill may be cynically exploited by the undeserving has caused that goodwill to virtually disappear in several European countries, with vociferous campaigns against (and vicious racial attacks on) asylum seekers.

In 2003, the INS was abolished and three separate agencies replaced it: U.S. Citizenship and Immigration Services, Immigration and Customs Enforcement (ICE), and Customs and Border Protection (CBP). All three agencies work under the umbrella of the Department of Homeland Security.

Text-Dependent Questions

1. What are the two primary reasons that immigrants come to the United States?
2. In which six states do the majority of legal immigrants tend to settle?
3. Approximately how much do illegal immigrants contribute in state and local taxes each year?

Research Projects

1. Why do the majority of immigrants come from Mexico, the People's Republic of China, the Philippines, India, and Vietnam?
2. If you were not already a U.S. citizen and wanted to move to the United States to live and work, what steps would you need to complete to become a legal immigrant?

CHAPTER 4
IMMIGRATION AND NATURALIZATION

This father with his daughter on his shoulders joined thousands of immigrants in a march for Immigrants and Mexicans against Illegal Immigration.

P rior to 2003, the Immigration and Naturalization Service (INS), an agency of the United States Department of Justice, was the office charged with the task of administering America's immigration laws. Prior to its inauguration, immigration itself was policed by the Immigration Bureau, while a separate Naturalization Service supervised the programs by which new immigrants took the steps to full naturalization as U.S. citizens.

The merger of these two agencies in 1933 offered clear administrative efficiencies, but it also exemplified a new and more imaginative official philosophy on the immigration issue. The new agency could take a longer, more positive view; although rigorously upholding the law, its agents could consider potential immigrants as individual men and women and families.

However, by 2003, it became clear that there needed to be better separation of duties and responsibilities with greater needs in all areas of the INS's oversight: citizenship and naturalization, customs enforcement, and border patrol. One agency was too unwieldy to handle the increased demand for oversight and tighter control and security. So the INS was replaced by three separate agencies. Rather than being a part of the Department of Justice, the three new agencies fell under administrative **jurisdiction** of the Department of Homeland Security. The three new agencies are U.S. Citizenship and Immigration Services (UCIS), Immigration and Customs Enforcement (ICE), and Customs and Border Protection (CBP). The UCIS is responsible for citizenship and naturalization, including for refugees and **asylees**. The ICE focuses on criminal and civil enforcement of federal laws governing border control, customs, trade, and

Words to Understand

Asylees: Refugees seeking entry to the United States.

Induction: Process of introducing and orienting new immigrants.

Jurisdiction: Power or right to govern an area.

immigration. The CBP's mission is to keep terrorists and their weapons out of the United States while facilitating lawful international travel and trade.

Justice for All: U.S. Citizenship and Immigration Services

The UCIS's goal is to be just and fair in their treatment of America's immigrants. Its 19,000 government employees and contractors working at 223 offices across the world oversee lawful immigration to the United States. The services it provides are citizenship, immigration of family members, work permits, verifying an individual's legal right to work in the United States, humanitarian programs (refugees and asylees), international adoptions, civic integration, and genealogy. One of the UCIS's missions is to help integrate immigrants into American civic culture.

According to the UCIS, on a typical day, the agency welcomes 3,200 new citizens. The organization also grants permanent residence to 4,000 people and issues 6,500 Permanent Resident Cards.

When it comes to national security, the UCIS does its part by performing nearly 148,000 national security background checks on an average day. It also fingerprints and photographs 15,000 applicants a day at its 136 Application Support Centers.

Administrating Citizenship

The UCIS's field offices across the United States handle the applications and associated work inside the country. Moreover, another 24 international offices are located in countries around the world. From Johannesburg to Frankfurt, from El Salvador to New Delhi, there are agents in place to oversee applications for immigration. The agency is thus in a position to be able to tackle many potential problems at the source, with incalculable benefits down the line for hard-pressed officials working on America's land frontiers and at its seaports and airports.

Those whose claims to a place in U.S. society seem good can have their passage smoothed, while those deemed undeserving can be dissuaded from embarking on a futile (and sometimes dangerous) journey. A properly managed admission procedure necessarily involves a good deal of paperwork—the more that can be taken care of beforehand the better for the immigrant. The new arrival in America will have quite enough to think about without having to undergo a protracted—and, at times, frustrating—**induction** process.

Humanitarian Programs

Since its reorganization in 2003, the UCIS has developed several humanitarian programs that provide protection to individuals in need of shelter due to disasters, oppression, and emergency medical situations. Programs include gaining refugee status, asylum, special immigrant juvenile status, and protection to human trafficking victims, among others. The common goal of each of these programs is to allow people in special need the ability to locate in the United States until the situation has been resolved or the person applies for permanent citizenship. In addition, the UCIS also assists families going through the international adoption process, to provide special services to young infants and children and their families.

Border Enforcement: Immigration and Customs Enforcement

The ICE, the second of the three new agencies formed when the INS dissolved, is the agency tasked with enforcing border control, customs, trade, and immigration.

As of 2016, the ICE had more than 20,000 employees in more than 400 offices across the United States and 46 countries outside the United States. With an annual budget of more than $6 billion, the ICE has been organized into four directorates. The two leading directorates are Enforcement and Removal Operations and Homeland Security Investigations. The other two directorates, Management and Administration and the Office of the Principal Legal Advisor, support the leading directorates. On an average day at the ICE, the agency makes 279 criminal alien arrests, including 4 human traffickers; 645 aliens are removed from the country, and more than 2,900 pounds of illegal narcotics are seized.

Enforcement and Removal

The Enforcement and Removal directorate employees are considered the backbone of the organization. They are the enforcers—the ones making arrests, detaining aliens, and seizing illegal drugs, currency, and assets. The ICE specializes in interior removals. These are removals of aliens already in the country, rather than people who are arrested during their efforts to enter the United States illegally.

In 2015 alone, the ICE successfully completed the removal of more than 235,000 aliens. Of these, 96,000 were noncriminal immigration violators, while nearly 140,000 were convicted criminals. More than 1,000 of the aliens were suspected or confirmed gang members. Beginning in 2015, the ICE began sharpening its focus to remove aliens who were identified as convicted criminals or those who posed a threat to public safety, rather than those who were simply violating immigration laws. Since those efforts began, the agency has seen a rise in the number of criminal aliens it has removed from the country.

The ICE is also responsible for the safe transport of all the people it removes from the country to their country of origin. The ICE uses its own Air Operations Unit to coordinate the transport of the people it removes. According to a 2015 report from the agency, the leading countries of origin of the people it has removed are Mexico, Guatemala, Honduras, and El Salvador.

Look behind the scenes as a Mexican people smuggler reveals the secrets of his trade.

Houston ICE Officers Send an El Salvadoran Gangster Home

On November 4, 2016, Edwin Antonio Torres, 27, a law enforcement fugitive and member of the Mara Salvatrucha (MS-13) gang from El Salvador, wanted for aggravated extortion and drug possession, was deported Friday by officers with U.S. Immigration and Customs Enforcement's (ICE) Enforcement and Removal Operations (ERO) in Houston. Torres, 27, was flown to El Salvador Nov. 4 onboard a charter flight coordinated by ICE's Air Operations (IAO) Unit. Upon arrival, Torres was turned over to officials from El Salvador's Civilian National Police (PNC). ERO officers discovered Torres when he was arrested in Texas for illegal possession of a weapon.

Border patrol agents on the U.S.–Mexico border intercepted 2,493 pounds of alleged marijuana that was concealed in a commercial shipment of fresh carrots.

The view of Algodones, Mexico, from the U.S. side of the border.

Border Patrol: Customs and Border Protection

The third new agency, the CBP, is responsible for keeping terrorists and their weapons out of the United States while facilitating lawful travel and trade in and out of the country. As of 2016, the CBP functioned with more than 60,000 employees and an annual budget of more than $12.4 billion. On one of its typical days, the CBP welcomes nearly one million visitors, screens more than 67,000 cargo containers, arrests more than 1,000 people, and seizes tons of illicit drugs.

Troy Newman to the Rescue

Racing through the Arizona Desert in an Agency 4×4, Agent Troy Newman brakes hard at the spot where a group of men has been found, quite clearly lost and exhausted. One has collapsed unconscious. In a temperature well over 100°F (38°C), this is no time to be walking across one of America's least hospitable regions. They are obviously illegal immigrants, but—as Troy explains to Tim Vanderpool of the *Christian Science Monitor*—there will be plenty of time for all those questions later. "Our goal here, first and foremost, is to respond to any emergencies," he says. Although ultimately an employee of the INS, Troy is first and foremost an emergency medical technician, a member of a BORSTAR—a Border Patrol Search, Trauma, and Rescue Team, a part of the CBP. There are around 100 EMTs in all, with outposts spread out along the Mexican border. Even so, it can be hard to help a person who has gone to some trouble not to be seen. Although more than 2,000 men and women were rescued in 2000 by teams like Troy's, many are never discovered—and with those that are, it is a race against time. "We always hope we can get to them while they're still alive," says Troy. "That's what our job is about."

Three Agencies, One Mission

Over the last several years, the previous roles of the INS have been adequately handled by these new agencies under the Homeland Security umbrella. With larger budgets and more workers focused on preventing terrorists and criminals from entering our borders, the UCIS, ICE, and CBP are up to the task and by all evidence succeeding. Since many of the UCIS's duties are administrative, the rest of this volume will focus on the work of the other two departments, Immigration and Customs Enforcement, and Customs and Border Protection.

Text-Dependent Questions

1. What three agencies replaced the INS?
2. Which agency is responsible for integrating immigrants into American culture?
3. Which directorate of the ICE is known as the enforcer of immigration laws and regulations?

Research Projects

1. Select one of the humanitarian programs operated by UCIS. Research how many people the program has helped and how many employees of the agency are involved in it.
2. Research how Customs and Border Protection works with other government entities such as the U.S. Coast Guard to protect the nation's borders, both on land and sea.

CHAPTER 5

A FOCUS ON CRIMINALS: IMMIGRATION AND CUSTOMS ENFORCEMENT

A view of the border fence between Arizona and Mexico.

D espite having more than 20,000 employees, by 2014 it became apparent to Immigration and Customs Enforcement (ICE) officials that these employees were stretched thin by seeking to apprehend all immigration law violators. In a report published in November 2014 called *Policies for the Apprehension, Detention, and Removal of Undocumented Immigrants*, the secretary of Homeland Security, Jeh Johnson, placed the highest priority on the removal of illegal aliens who, in addition to breaking immigration laws were also threats to national security, border security, and public safety. With this focus, the agency removed fewer people in 2015, but the percentage of convicted felons increased—59 percent of all removals were people who had previously been convicted of a crime.

Since its inception in 2003, the ICE has both sharpened its focus and refined its officers' skills and operations. Efficient leadership is one reason for the agency's continued success.

At the Top

The ICE's top leader is its director, Sarah Saldaña. Saldaña was formerly a U.S. attorney for the Northern District of Texas. Saldaña depends on the leadership of Daniel Ragsdale for overseeing the day-to-day operations of the agency. His title, deputy director, reflects his position, but not his duties. As COO, he depends on the assistance from the next leader in the chain of command, the chief of staff, Leonard Joseph. These three top executives of the agency are called upon to ensure it is accomplishing its mission as dictated by the secretary of the Department of Homeland Security.

Words to Understand

Biometric identification: Uses genetic traits, such as fingerprints and voice waves, to identify a person.

Collateral: Accompanying as secondary or subordinate.

Repatriation: The return of someone to his or her own country.

This mission includes enforcing more than 400 federal statutes and focuses on smart immigration enforcement, preventing terrorism, and combating the illegal movement of people and goods. It takes precise organization and coordination between departments and officers to achieve the agency's goals.

Organized for Efficiency

The two primary directorates of the ICE are Enforcement and Removal Operations (ERO) and Homeland Security Investigations. As mentioned, ERO is responsible for the identification, arrest, and removal of aliens who present a danger to the nation's security or public safety. ERO is then further divided into these departments for sharper focus of responsibilities: Custody Management, Enforcement, Field Operations, ICE Health Service Corps, Operations Support, and Removal.

Introduction to Immigration and Customs Enforcement (ICE).

- **Custody Management:** manages ICE detention operations efficiently and effectively to provide security, safety, and care of aliens in custody.
- **Enforcement:** divided into three programs:
  - Criminal Alien, which provides direction and support in the biometric identification, arrest, and removal of priority aliens;
  - National Fugitive Operations, which focuses on reducing the fugitive alien population in the United States; and
  - Priority Enforcement, which enables the Department of Homeland Security to work with state and local enforcement to take custody of those who pose a danger to the public.

Immigration and Customs Enforcement deports a Brazilian fugitive wanted for his role in a murder-for-hire. The agents' faces were blurred in order to protect their identity.

- Field Operations: coordinates enforcement and removal efforts through 24 field offices.
- Health Service Corps: provides direct patient care.
- Operations Support provides the necessary resources and infrastructure to support the ERO mission.

Homeland Security Investigations (HSI) is made up of the following departments:

- Domestic Operations: oversees the HSI's domestic field operations.
- International Property Rights (IPR) Center: responds to international property theft.
- Information Management: improves methods for managing different types of information and how that information is shared.
- International Operations: Homeland Security's largest investigative presence overseas, which provides assistance with investigations and repatriation efforts.
- Investigative Programs Division: oversees HSI's diverse planning and operational initiatives and oversees the application of national law enforcement policy to HSI operations.
- National Security Investigations Division: leads its effort to combat criminal enterprises by investigating vulnerabilities in the nation's border, infrastructure, and economic and transportation systems.
- HSI's Office of Intelligence: Develops intelligence on illegal trade, travel, and financial activity and shares this information with field offices and law enforcement partners worldwide.
- HSI's Mission Support Division: manages critical functions that support the efficient use of HSI resources and manages functions that support HSI's strategic goals and performance measures.

A Customs and Border Patrol agent with the canine division.

On the Trail

A cut strand of barbed wire here, a bent or broken fencepost there: often, the visible signs of entry are only too clear. The experienced sign cutter, however, can also "read" the rocky ground like a book. A glance or two is enough to confirm the passage of people—and, frequently, their number and their rate of progress. There are five main types of trace.

The first is the flattening effect of a footstep or vehicle squashing down rocks, dirt, or twigs into the desert earth. The second is any sign of regularity, which is never found in nature: the circles and other geometrical shapes left by the typical trainer-sole or tire practically scream out to the experienced tracker. The third thing to look for is any disturbance: the dislodging of stones or twigs from their proper place is clear evidence that somebody has recently passed this way. Next comes color change: disturbed rock, soil, or vegetation tends to catch the light differently, and often this is all that sharp-eyed sign cutters need to see to know they are on the trail. The fifth characteristic is transfer: anything moved out of place by a passing shoe, such as when rich mud from a ditch or arroyo turns up in an area of arid sand.

A footprint may show up in some lights, but be entirely invisible in others. The tracker learns to examine the ground carefully from a number of different angles. Some times of day are better than others. In the early morning, for instance, the disturbance of dew on grass and low shrubs may be a giveaway sign. Since certain surfaces take better tracks than others, what has been a reasonably clear trail may abruptly disappear. Those tracks that can be identified are carefully flagged with little bits of toilet paper tied to twigs, and these may help direction to be maintained until footprints can once again be seen.

The identification of such immediate physical traces is the central skill of sign cutting, but trackers with talent and experience can "read" a good many more. Some may be as obvious as a discarded water bottle or candy bar wrapper, but others are harder to pin down. Ideally, sign cutters learn to think themselves into the mind of the illegal immigrant. Men and women walking across country tend to take the path of least resistance—in rough terrain, it is often possible to guess their likely route with a fair degree of confidence. In a largely featureless landscape, unguided wayfarers have a tendency to take aim on some distant landmark. Again, the intuitive tracker may be able to accurately predict their course.

A Day in the Life of Those at Immigration and Customs Enforcement

On an average day at the ICE, the following activities take place, among other important functions:

- ERO houses an average of 34,260 illegal aliens in these various facilities nationwide.
- ERO personnel manages over 1.71 million aliens in the various stages of immigration removal proceedings.

Part of the border fence separating the United States and Mexico.

- ERO processes 1,305 aliens into detention centers.
- ERO health care professionals conduct approximately 603 intake health care screenings in facilities staffed by ERO health care providers.
- ERO removes 1,120 aliens from the United States to countries around the globe, including 616 criminal aliens.

A masked and armed special forces soldier stands ready to face drug cartels near the violence-ridden border city of Ciudad Juarez, Mexico.

Volunteer Rapid Response Teams Go Extra Mile to Help Others

One way that the ICE prepares to assist during natural or human-made disasters is through its rapid response teams (RRTs). According to the ICE's website, many HSI RRTs have a specialization. San Diego RRT is trained to navigate tunnels and confined spaces under emergency conditions. Los Angeles RRT specializes in search and rescue (SAR) operations. Commander and Group Supervisor John R. Reynolds said, "Seventeen members of

U.S. Customs and Border Protection rescues illegal immigrants stranded on a steep cliff in a UH-60 Blackhawk helicopter.

our team are SAR certified technicians, level two. We focus on wilderness search and rescue, but also have the capability to search urban areas." The team's primary training partner for SAR operations is the Los Angeles County Sheriff's Department, Malibu Search and Rescue Team. In 2014, the Los Angeles RRT worked for three days with Ventura County SAR looking for a firefighter from Arcadia, CA, who went missing while hiking in a remote area near Fillmore, CA. His body was located several weeks later.

In addition to search and rescue expertise, the team also possesses a wealth of medical knowledge. There are four emergency medical technicians on the team, and two are ICE-certified Tactical Medics. They received training from an ICE-endorsed program in conjunction with Johns Hopkins University.

The HSI RRT Los Angeles is staffed entirely with volunteers, the majority of whom are HSI special agents and administrative personnel for support. Los Angeles has 27 members on its team. Each person must train a minimum of 96 hours per year to remain an active member, though many put in more than 200 hours annually. ICE HSI allows agents to dedicate a portion of their regular workload to RRT training and serve as a **collateral** duty.

Frontline: Andalucía

Five would-be immigrants a day are believed to drown in the Straits of Gibraltar in the attempt to make the crossing from impoverished Africa to affluent Europe. Although only a few miles wide, the straits are rendered treacherous by swift currents and by the busy traffic of one of the world's most important shipping lanes.

Organized gangs of people smugglers charge migrants between $600 and $1,000 a time for a place in a small boat so full of passengers that it may well ride less than 12 inches (30 cm) above the waterline. Many inevitably founder or overturn, but there is still no shortage of prospective passengers: the economics of emigration are just too appealing.

Most come from Morocco, although there is also a steady stream from sub-Saharan Africa. They and their families will have saved for years to earn this precarious passage. Those who make it as far as Spain will find themselves at the very bottom of the social heap, toiling long hours in agriculture at half the wages of native-born Spanish farmworkers. A dismal prospect? Not from their perspective. That rate of pay works out to be 10 times what they could hope to earn at home in North Africa. Many of the migrants save money to send home to their family.

In what has long been one of Spain's poorest areas, there have been several serious outbreaks of racial violence among the local population, but, despite the difficulties, the rewards for the immigrants are just too great to be resisted, and the problem is likely to continue for many years.

Text-Dependent Questions

1. What are the two primary directorates of the ICE?
2. What does the HSI's Mission Support Division do?
3. How many aliens in various stages of removal do ICE employees manage on an average day?

Research Projects

1. Research the ICE detention center closest to you. How many people are housed there on an average day?
2. What rapid response team is located closest to you? How often has it been deployed and during which disasters?

CHAPTER 6

CUSTOMS
AND BORDER
PROTECTION

Border patrol agents received information regarding a stash house. Fifty-two immigrants from different countries and five smugglers were arrested. Border patrol agents and officers from three different counties conducted a joint investigation leading them to the residence. Faces are blurred to protect the people's identities.

** America's borders," said a White House statement issued in January 2002, "are the boundaries between the United States and the rest of the world." That may seem like a statement of the obvious, and yet it is by no means immediately clear how the nation is to address the paradox that President George W. Bush's press office went on to pinpoint so precisely. On the one hand, as it said, "The massive flow of people and goods across our borders helps drive our economy." On the other, "It can also serve as a conduit for terrorists, weapons of mass destruction, illegal migrants, contraband, and other unlawful commodities."

The very next year, the Bureau of Customs and Border Protection (CBP) was formed, making it the first joint border management agency in the world, and the largest federal law enforcement agency in the United States. Its scope is no small one. On an average day at the CBP, more than one million passengers pass through the nation's borders, which makes the number of its employees—more than 54,000 employees—a reasonable number. Plus, the agency is also responsible for keeping all ports of trade safe and secure. It takes a focus on organization and knowledge of responsibilities to keep such a large agency operating efficiently.

Efficient Operations

More than a dozen departments make up the CBP. While some of them, like **Enterprise** Services, provide administrative services to the agency, others are hard at work to meet the agency's mission: keeping terrorists and their weapons out of the United States while facilitating

Words to Understand

Collaboration: Working with another person or group to achieve something.

Enterprise: A business organization.

Interdiction: Prevention of illegal person or goods from entering the country.

Border patrol officers working together at the Center's headquarters in California.

lawful international travel and trade. The top departments carrying out that mission include Air and Marine Operations, Office of Field Operations, U.S. Border Patrol, and the Office of Trade. To understand how large the agency is, Field Operations alone operates 20 major field offices, 328 ports of entry, and 70 locations in more than 40 countries internationally.

In its report "Vision and Strategy 2020," the CBP's strategic plan for the future, the agency outlined three main strategic themes that will be the focus of all the departments of the agency:

Collaboration: According to the report, improved **collaboration** throughout the CBP and with its stakeholders provides a shared sense of purpose, enhanced understanding of the operating environment, increased trust, and complementary engagement.

Innovation: The CBP is committed to leveraging science, technology, and corporate innovation to ensure optimal capabilities development for peak performance.

Integration: The CBP says it must lead development of a seamless global network to integrate border enforcement capabilities and meet the demands of a constantly evolving landscape.

Specializing in Safety

When CBP offices seek to focus on a specific issue in their area, they form task forces. These task forces become experts on the issue at hand and often can bring about more effective results. This is certainly true of a CBP task force in Southern California, the Priority One Task Force (POTF) of Indio, CA. POTF's focus was on apprehending convicted criminals who were illegally crossing the border. This same focus has been a big part of Immigration and Customs Enforcement's (ICE's) efforts as well.

POTF has met its goals exceptionally well. Since its inception on April 5, 2015, Indio POTF agents have arrested 110 career-criminal illegal aliens convicted for murder, kidnapping, sex offenses, gang crimes, assault with a deadly weapon, a wide variety of narcotics crimes, child cruelty, domestic violence, fraud, burglary, DUI, and petty and grand theft.

A Day in the Life of Customs and Border Patrol

Protecting the borders is all in a day's job for the more than 59,000 employees of the CBP. While no day is really typical, here are some average numbers for 2016 indicating the CBP's activities and effectiveness on any given day during the year:

- Processed 282,252 privately owned vehicles
- Conducted 924 apprehensions between U.S. ports of entry.
- Arrested 23 wanted criminals at U.S. ports of entry
- Refused 367 inadmissible persons at U.S. ports of entry
- Discovered 470 pests at U.S. ports of entry and 4,548 materials for quarantine —plant, meat, animal byproduct, and soil
- Seized 9,435 pounds of drugs, $356,396 in undeclared or illicit currency, and $3.7 million dollars' worth of products with intellectual property rights violations
- Identified 600 individuals with suspected national security concerns

Visit the Border Patrol Boot Camp in Artesia, NM. It's considered to be the toughest of any military or government service training.

U.S. Customs and Border Patrol Office of Field Operations officers working in Norfolk, VA, seized stolen vehicles and automobile parts valued at approximately $85,000.

Planning for the Future with Technology

Technology is a key ingredient of the CBP's success, and the agency is acutely aware of that. It has invested in several technologies that have improved efficiencies and allowed the agency to achieve its operational goals.

One example of this is the $11 million expansion of the Air and Marine Operations Center (AMOC) located at March Air Reserve Base in Riverside, CA. The AMOC is an international, multidomain federal law enforcement operations center that uses sophisticated technology to detect, identify, track, and direct the **interdiction** of suspect aviation and maritime targets wherever they are discovered.

The exterior and interior of the Customs and Border Patrol Air and Marine Operations Center on the March Air Reserve Base in Riverside, CA.

The project should take approximately one year to complete and will house information technology equipment and staff, administrative offices, conference and break-out rooms, and secure storage, while also providing space to additional law enforcement liaisons.

Another example of the CBP's use of technology is its Mobile Passport Control (MPC) system. Mobile Passport is the first authorized app to expedite a traveler's arrival into the United States. Eligible travelers may voluntarily submit their passport information and answers to inspection-related questions to CBP via a smartphone or tablet app prior to arrival.

MPC currently offers U.S. citizens and Canadian visitors a more efficient in-person inspection between the CBP officer and the traveler upon arrival in the United States. Much like Automated Passport Control (APC) the app does not require preapproval and is free to use. Travelers who successfully use the app will no longer have to complete a paper form or use an APC kiosk. As a result, travelers will experience shorter wait times, less congestion, and faster processing. The MPC pilot launched in August 2014 for eligible travelers arriving at Hartsfield-Jackson Atlanta International Airport, and has since expanded to 18 airports.

It could be said that no other agency of the U.S. government has been affected more by September 11, 2001, than the CBP, as well as the other two branches of service that replaced the Immigration and Naturalization Service. Over the last several years these agencies have effectively guarded our land, sea, and air borders, keeping us as safe as possible from terrorist attacks.

Text-Dependent Questions

1. Approximately how many people work for the CBP?
2. On a typical day, how many wanted criminals does the CBP arrest at U.S. ports of entry?
3. What is MPC technology?

Research Projects

1. Find a CBP field office near you. How many people work there, and what border is it responsible for guarding?
2. Find the 18 airports currently using MPC technology. How many passengers have used the technology and how does it make customs inspection easier for both passengers and CBP officers?

Series Glossary

Air marshal: Armed guard traveling on an aircraft to protect the passengers and crew; the air marshal is often disguised as a passenger.

Annexation: To incorporate a country or other territory within the domain of a state.

Armory: A supply of arms for defense or attack.

Assassinate: To murder by sudden or secret attack, usually for impersonal reasons.

Ballistic: Of or relating to firearms.

Biological warfare: Also known as germ warfare, this is war fought with biotoxins—harmful bacteria or viruses that are artificially propagated and deliberately dispersed to spread sickness among an enemy.

Cartel: A combination of groups with a common action or goal.

Chemical warfare: The use of poisonous or corrosive substances to kill or incapacitate the enemy; it differs from biological warfare in that the chemicals concerned are not organic, living germs.

Cold War: A long and bitter enmity between the United States and the Free World and the Soviet Union and its Communist satellites, which went on from 1945 to the collapse of Communism in 1989.

Communism: A system of government in which a single authoritarian party controls state-owned means of production.

Conscription: Compulsory enrollment of persons especially for military service.

Consignment: A shipment of goods or weapons.

Contingency operations: Operations of a short duration and most often performed at short notice, such as dropping supplies into a combat zone.

Counterintelligence: Activities designed to collect information about enemy espionage and then to thwart it.

Covert operations: Secret plans and activities carried out by spies and their agencies.

Cyberterrorism: A form of terrorism that seeks to cause disruption by interfering with computer networks.

Democracy: A government elected to rule by the majority of a country's people.

Depleted uranium: One of the hardest known substances, it has most of its radioactivity removed before being used to make bullets.

Dissident: A person who disagrees with an established religious or political system, organization, or belief.

Embargo: A legal prohibition on commerce.

Emigration: To leave one country to move to another country.

Extortion: The act of obtaining money or other property from a person by means of force or intimidation.

Extradite: To surrender an alleged criminal from one state or nation to another having jurisdiction to try the charge.

Federalize/federalization: The process by which National Guard units, under state command in normal circumstances, are called up by the president in times of crisis to serve the federal government of the United States as a whole.

Genocide: The deliberate and systematic destruction of a racial, political, or cultural group.

Guerrilla: A person who engages in irregular warfare, especially as a member of an independent unit carrying out harassment and sabotage.

Hijack: To take unlawful control of a ship, train, aircraft, or other form of transport.

Immigration: The movement of a person or people ("immigrants") into a country; as opposed to emigration, their movement out.

Indict: To charge with a crime by the finding or presentment of a jury (as a grand jury) in due form of law.

Infiltrate: To penetrate an organization, like a terrorist network.

Infrastructure: The crucial networks of a nation, such as transportation and communication, and also including government organizations, factories, and schools.

Insertion: Getting into a place where hostages are being held.

Insurgent: A person who revolts against civil authority or an established government.

Internment: To hold someone, especially an immigrant, while his or her application for residence is being processed.

Logistics: The aspect of military science dealing with the procurement, maintenance, and transportation of military matériel, facilities, and personnel.

Matériel: Equipment, apparatus, and supplies used by an organization or institution.

Militant: Having a combative or aggressive attitude.

Militia: a military force raised from civilians, which supports a regular army in times of war.

Narcoterrorism: Outrages arranged by drug trafficking gangs to destabilize government, thus weakening law enforcement and creating conditions for the conduct of their illegal business.

NATO: North Atlantic Treaty Organization; an organization of North American and European countries formed in 1949 to protect one another against possible Soviet aggression.

Naturalization: The process by which a foreigner is officially "naturalized," or accepted as a U.S. citizen.

Nonstate actor: A terrorist who does not have official government support.

Ordnance: Military supplies, including weapons, ammunition, combat vehicles, and maintenance tools and equipment.

Refugee: A person forced to take refuge in a country not his or her own, displaced by war or political instability at home.

Rogue state: A country, such as Iraq or North Korea, that ignores the conventions and laws set by the international community; rogue states often pose a threat, either through direct military action or by harboring terrorists.

Sortie: One mission or attack by a single plane.

Sting: A plan implemented by undercover police in order to trap criminals.

Surveillance: To closely watch over and monitor situations; the USAF employs many different kinds of surveillance equipment and techniques in its role as an intelligence gatherer.

Truce: A suspension of fighting by agreement of opposing forces.

UN: United Nations; an international organization, of which the United States is a member, that was established in 1945 to promote international peace and security.

Chronology

1865: Individual states start passing their own piecemeal legislation imposing laws and limits on immigration; prior to this, no serious attempt had been made to control the flow.

1875: Supreme Court decides that the regulation of immigration is the responsibility of federal, rather than state, government.

1882: Chinese Exclusion Act bars entry to Chinese immigrants for a 10-year period.

1891: Immigration Act bars polygamists and "persons convicted of crimes of moral turpitude" from admission to the United States, along with individuals suffering from dangerously contagious diseases. Immigration Service set up to police the new rules.

1892: January 2, Federal Immigration Station at Ellis Island, New York Harbor, opens.

1906: Basic Naturalization Act standardizes the naturalization process U.S.-wide, bringing it out of state and into federal control; Naturalization Service is set up to administer procedures.

1917: Immigration Act sets minimum literacy standards for all immigrants, demanding that they be able to read and write in their own language; in practice, this favors middle-class European immigrants with good levels of education.

1921: Immigration Act, known as the Quota Act, stipulates that new immigrants can be admitted only in numbers proportional to their representation in earlier census findings; this clearly favors those belonging to long-established—and mainly European— ethnic communities.

1924: Immigration Act, known as the Johnson-Reed Act, reinforces the provisions of the Immigration Act of 1921. Illegal immigration rises throughout this period, as possibilities for legal entry are progressively foreclosed.

1933: Immigration Service and Naturalization Service merge into a single Immigration and Naturalization Service (INS).

1941–1945: America is involved in Second World War; INS is in charge of detaining "aliens" (especially Japanese Americans) in internment camps and guarding borders against enemy spies.

1950: Statute of the United Nations High Commissioner for Refugees passed by resolution of UN General Assembly; it stipulates that those with a "well-founded fear of persecution" have a legal right to claim protection.

1986: Immigration Reform and Control Act lets INS act against employers found to have hired undocumented aliens; since the law also gives certain illegal aliens the opportunity of regularizing their position, it is seen as representing a decisive shift toward a more compassionate immigration policy.

2003: INS is dissolved and replaced by three agencies: U.S. Citizenship and Immigration Services, Immigration and Customs Enforcement (ICE), and Customs and Border Protection (CBP).

June 2003: The Public Health Security and Bioterrorism Preparedness and Response Act is enacted requiring prior notification to the CBP and the U.S. Food and Drug Administration (FDA) of food imports.

2004: U.S. Visitor and Immigrant Status Indicator Technology (US-VISIT) program is instituted in the 50 busiest land border ports of entry. It provides visa-issuing posts and ports of entry with biometric technology that allows a traveler's identity to be established and verified.

2016: On Wednesday, February 24, 2016, President Obama signed the Trade Facilitation and Trade Enforcement Act of 2015. Also known as the Customs Reauthorization Bill, this was the first reauthorization for the CBP since its creation within the Department of Homeland Security in 2003.

Further Resources

Websites

U.S. Citizenship and Immigration Services: www.uscis.gov

U.S. Immigration and Customs Enforcement: www.ice.gov

U.S. Customs and Border Patrol: www.cbp.gov

Further Reading

Various books celebrate America's modern diversity and multicultural history.

Broyles, Bill, and Haynes, Mark. *Desert Duty: On the Line with the U.S. Border Patrol.* Austin: University of Texas Press, 2010.

Daniels, Roger. *Coming to America: A History of Immigration and Ethnicity in American Life.* New York: HarperCollins, 1990.

Elmore, Rocky. *Out on Foot: Nightly Patrols and Ghostly Tales of a U.S. Border Patrol Agent.* National Harbor, MD: Duffin Creative, 2015.

Graham Gaines, Ann. *Border Patrol Agent and Careers in Border Protection* (Homeland Security and Counterterrorism Careers). New York, NY: Enslow Publishing, 2006.

Pipher, Mary Bray. *The Middle of Everywhere: The World's Refugees Come to Our Town.* New York: Harcourt Brace, 2002. This is right up-to-date with an inspiring account of the contribution made by new Americans from as far afield as Iraq, Sudan, and the former Soviet Union to the author's home city in the heart of America, Lincoln, NE.

Takaki, Ronald T. *A Different Mirror: A History of Multicultural America.* Boston: Little, Brown, 1993. This draws on everything from folk songs and letters to ensure that the different ethnic traditions find full representation.

Takaki, Ronald T. *A Larger Memory: A History of Our Diversity, with Voices.* Boston: Little, Brown, 1998. This is an anthology of personal testimony from throughout American history and across the entire American ethnic spectrum.

Index

About the Author

Michael Kerrigan was born in Liverpool, England, and educated at St. Edward's College, from where he won an Open Scholarship to University College, Oxford. He lived for a time in the United States, spending time first at Princeton, followed by a period working in publishing in New York. Since then he has been a freelance writer and journalist, with commissions across a very wide range of subjects, but with a special interest in social policy and defense issues. Within this field, he has written on every region of the world. His work has been published by leading international educational publishers, including the BBC, Dorling Kindersley, Time-Life, and Reader's Digest Books. His work as a journalist includes regular contributions to the *Times Literary Supplement*, London, as well as a weekly column in the *Scotsman* newspaper, Edinburgh, where he now lives with his wife and their two small children.

About the Consultant

Manny Gomez, an expert on terrorism and security, is President of MG Security Services and a former Principal Relief Supervisor and Special Agent with the FBI. He investigated terrorism and espionage cases as an agent in the National Security Division. He was a certified undercover agent and successfully completed Agent Survival School. Chairman of the Board of the National Law Enforcement Association (NLEA), Manny is also a former Sergeant in the New York Police Department (NYPD) where he supervised patrol and investigative activities of numerous police officers, detectives, and civilian personnel. Mr. Gomez worked as a uniformed and plainclothes officer in combating narcotics trafficking, violent crimes, and quality of life concerns. He has executed over 100 arrests and received departmental recognition on eight separate occasions. Mr. Gomez has a bachelor's degree and a master's degree and is a graduate of Fordham University School of Law where he was on the dean's list. He is admitted to the New York and New Jersey Bar. He served honorably in the United States Marine Corps infantry.